SHARKS!

PHONICS

What Is That Smell?

Book 7: s-blends

By Quinlan B. Lee

Photo Credits: cover: Jeff Hunter/Getty Images; title page: Mattias Klum/Corbis; pages 2-3: Charles Steele/National Geographic; pages 4-5: Jeff Hunter/Getty Images; pages 6-7: Louise Murray/Alamy; pages 8-9: Mattias Klum/Corbis; pages 10-11: Stephen Frink/Corbis; pages 12-13: George Karbus Photography/cultura/Corbis; page 14: Luis Javier Sandoval/Getty Images; page 16: Valerie Potapova/Shutterstock.

12 11 10 9 8 7   7 18/0

D1092619

First Printing, September 2014

SCHOLASTIC INC.

You have five senses.
But sharks have six
strong senses.

They can see, **smell**, hear, taste, touch, and sense electricity.

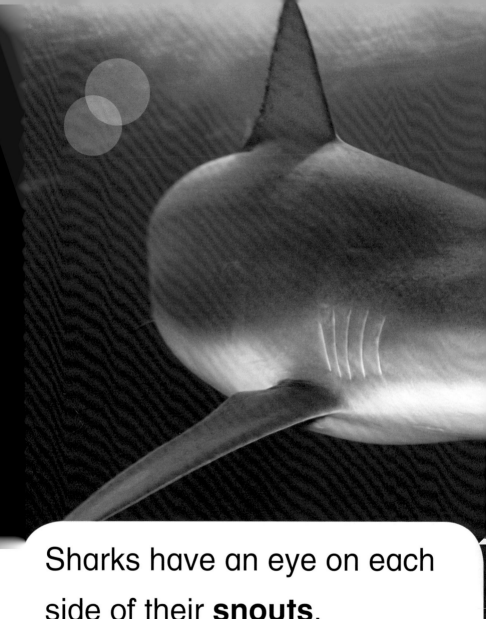

Sharks have an eye on each side of their **snouts**.
They **stare** out into the water.

Sharks can **spot** prey in the dark and in the deep.

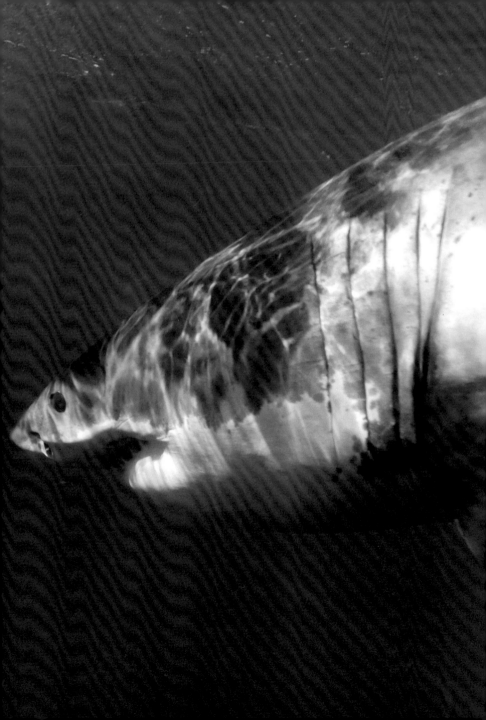

Sharks **smell** with **small slits** on the side of their **snouts**. They can **smell** blood from miles away. They can even **sniff** a **small** drop.

Sharks have very **small** ears. But they can even hear the **small**, low sounds that fish make.

Sharks have **small** tubes in their **skin** that help them feel. There is a **strip** of tubes down their sides.

If a fish **swims** by them, they feel the **swish**. Then they **snatch** the fish and eat it.

Sharks can taste, too.
They will **sneak** a **small** bite
of prey first.

If it does not taste right, then they will **stay** away and not eat it.

All animals have an electric field around them.

Sharks can sense them!

They have **small** holes in their **snouts** that can feel the electricity.

This helps them **sneak** up on prey.

All of a shark's **strong** senses help make it a **strong** predator.